Thomas Jefferson

Victoria Sherrow

LERNER PUBLICATIONS COMPANY • MINNEAPOLIS

For my sister Marianne, with love

Illustrations by Tim Parlin

Text copyright © 2002 by Victoria Sherrow
Illustrations copyright © 2002 by Lerner Publications Company

Lerner Publications Company
A division of Lerner Publishing Group
241 First Avenue North
Minneapolis, MN 55401 U.S.A.

Website address: www.lernerbooks.com

Library of Congress Cataloging-in-Publication Data

Sherrow, Victoria.
    Thomas Jefferson / by Victoria Sherrow.
        p.   cm. — (History maker bios)
    Includes bibliographical references (p.   ) and index.
    Summary: An introduction to the life of Thomas Jefferson, discussing his roles as drafter of the Declaration of Independence, ambassador to France, secretary of state, vice president, and president of the United States of America.
    ISBN: 0–8225–0197–X (lib. bdg. : alk. paper)
    1. Jefferson, Thomas, 1743–1826—Juvenile literature. 2. Presidents— United States—Biography—Juvenile literature. [1. Jefferson, Thomas, 1743–1826. 2. Presidents.] I. Title. II. Series.
E332.79 .S54 2002
973.4'6'092—dc21   2001003832

Manufactured in the United States of America
1 2 3 4 5 6 – JR – 07 06 05 04 03 02

TABLE OF CONTENTS

INTRODUCTION

Thomas Jefferson was a great American thinker and leader. He wrote most of the Declaration of Independence. And he served the new United States of America as secretary of state, vice president, and then president.

Jefferson's ideas are at the heart of the Declaration of Independence: All men are created equal. All people are born with the rights to life, liberty, and the pursuit of happiness. No ruler can take these rights away. These ideas have become part of the way Americans think and live. Jefferson's words have also inspired people all over the world.

This is his story.

1 COUNTRY ROOTS

Thomas Jefferson grew up with a deep love for the land. He was born on a plantation called Shadwell in western Virginia on April 13, 1743. This area was known as the frontier. It was newly settled land and was rich in forests, rivers, and mountains.

Young Tom learned to paddle a canoe on the nearby rivers. He learned about planting and harvesting crops. And he went fishing and horseback riding. Tom's father told his son that those who were strong in body were also strong and free in mind.

Tom looked up to his father. Peter Jefferson had made his own way as a farmer. He did not have much schooling as a child but educated himself by reading. Using his talents and hard work, he had become successful.

Tom spent his early childhood and some of his teenage years at Shadwell. He and his family lived on a nearby plantation called Tuckahoe for the seven years in between.

Like his father, Tom was tall, with large hands and feet, freckles, and hazel eyes. His friends called him Tall Tom. Tom also had a head of thick red hair.

Father and son shared a love of books. Tom could already read and write when he started school at age five. Four years later, he began studying Latin, Greek, and French to prepare for college. His friends sometimes teased him because he would not play outside until he finished all his schoolwork.

Tom's love of reading lasted a lifetime. He once said, "I cannot live without books."

In his private notebook, Tom copied down the words of his favorite poets and writers.

Tom also kept a private notebook. He filled page after page with descriptions of plants, animals, and the weather. He copied down his favorite poems and ideas. Peter Jefferson encouraged Tom to keep learning new things.

When Tom was fourteen years old, his life changed. That year, Peter Jefferson died. Tom later said his father's death had left him without a relative or friend who could guide him.

As a young man, Tom wanted to do what would have made his father proud. Above all, he wanted a fine education.

Thomas Jefferson said that music was the favorite passion of his soul.

In 1760, Tom entered the College of William and Mary in Williamsburg, the capital of Virginia at that time. At about six feet two inches tall, Thomas Jefferson towered over the other students. He was shy around large groups, but people admired his fine manners. He could dance well and play the violin. Among friends, he showed his keen sense of humor. And he always had something interesting to say.

Thomas took his college studies very seriously. He often spent fifteen hours a day reading. He graduated with top honors at age twenty.

After college, Thomas studied law for five years with George Wythe. He admired Wythe and called his teacher his second father. He often visited Wythe's brick home with its fine library.

Thomas's teacher encouraged him to make a schedule for each day and follow it. That way he would not waste any time. Thomas took the advice to heart. He scheduled his entire day, from the time he got up at dawn to the time he went to bed at night.

Thomas called George Wythe his faithful and beloved teacher. The two men became lifelong friends.

By 1766, Thomas had more on his mind than his studies. He was also thinking about politics. The Virginia House of Burgesses met in Williamsburg. They were the elected lawmakers for the colony. As a British settlement, the colony of Virginia had to follow the laws made by Great Britain. But its House of Burgesses could also make some laws of its own.

Jefferson often stood in the doorway of the House of Burgesses and listened to the men discuss new laws and ways to govern Virginia. Some of these men were angry with the king of Britain.

SUNRISE TO SUNSET

Thomas Jefferson began each morning by soaking his feet in cold water. He then read his law books, ran two miles, rode his horse, and practiced his violin. Jefferson carried a pencil and notebook in his pocket so he could keep track of his schedule and jot down ideas wherever he went.

King George III was crowned the ruler of Great Britain in 1760. He and his taxes were not very popular with the colonists.

The king had allowed Britain to begin taxing the colonists without their agreement. Britain passed taxes on tea and other items shipped from Britain.

Many colonists did not want to pay these taxes. Jefferson agreed. Why should a small island thousands of miles away tell people in the colonies how to live? And why should the colonists have to obey a king whom no one had elected?

By 1767, Thomas had finished his studies and become a lawyer. He proved to be good at his job and had plenty of work. But he was also becoming more and more interested in the work of government.

2 CALLED TO SERVE

In December 1768, Jefferson was elected to the Virginia House of Burgesses. He and the other lawmakers did not always agree on how to run Virginia. They did agree on one thing, though—British taxes. They still thought the taxes were unfair.

Busy as he was, Jefferson made time for new projects. Lately he had begun making plans to build a home for himself. Since childhood, he had wanted to live at the top of a hill on his father's land. Jefferson would call his new home Monticello, the Italian word for "little mountain."

Jefferson had read many books about architecture around the world. And he was especially interested in architecture from Italy. He was designing his Monticello to be unlike any other home in America.

Jefferson made this drawing of his dream home. He wanted to design and help build Monticello himself.

Putting Up and Pulling Down

Jefferson once said that architecture was his delight and that putting up and pulling down was one of his favorite amusements. For forty years, Jefferson found ways to improve Monticello, inside and out. At one point, he decided to tear most of the house down and start all over. That way he could add a dome to his house. He was just as picky about his garden. Like the house, his garden was always changing and improving.

When Jefferson fell in love with Martha Wayles Skelton, it seemed he had found someone to share Monticello with. Martha loved to read and shared Thomas's passion for music. She was also pretty and kindhearted. The two married on New Year's Day in 1772. The main house at Monticello was not finished, so the couple moved into a small building nearby.

Several years after his marriage, Jefferson stopped practicing law. Instead he devoted himself to the work of government. The colonies were still angry with Britain. And the British still told them what they could and could not do.

A growing number of colonists believed the American colonies should be a free nation. Some were willing to go to war for this freedom. Other colonists wanted independence but worried that the Americans could not win a war. Still others supported Britain.

In 1773, colonists organized the Boston Tea Party. They dumped British tea into Boston Harbor to protest taxes.

Jefferson shared his own views with the House of Burgesses. He was not a good public speaker. But he was a powerful writer. Jefferson put into words his dream of a free America. He wrote about democracy—government by the people. In a democracy, people could choose their own leaders and lawmakers.

Some of the men who read Jefferson's ideas decided to publish them. Soon his words were read all over the colonies.

Jefferson was not one to give long speeches. "In cases of doubt it is better to say too little than too much," was his advice.

His ideas were new to people who were used to being ruled by kings and queens. But many colonists were inspired by Jefferson's words.

By the spring of 1775, the colonists were doing more than just talking about freedom. On April 19, British and American soldiers fought battles in Massachusetts at Lexington and Concord. These battles marked the start of the Revolutionary War.

That fall, Jefferson joined other colonial leaders in Philadelphia for the Second Continental Congress. The Congress was made up of representatives from nearly all the colonies. It was their job to decide how to unite all the colonies in a war for their freedom.

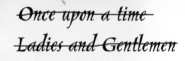

Once upon a time
Ladies and Gentlemen
Hey everybody
In ^the course of human events...?

THE
DECLARATION OF
INDEPENDENCE

In June 1776, the Continental Congress voted to declare America free from British rule. They chose Thomas Jefferson to write this statement. He was not as experienced as some of the other representatives. But the other representatives knew he was a skilled writer.

Jefferson had rented two rooms in a brick home just outside Philadelphia. Each day, he sat in one of the rooms before a folding writing box he had designed himself. He spent many hours a day writing and rewriting. Every single word had to be just the right one. Jefferson put his heartfelt ideas about liberty and justice into the document. He worked on it for nearly three weeks.

Jefferson designed his writing box to do many things. It could be used as a reading desk and a writing desk. It could also be closed up and used to carry papers and books.

Jefferson wrote and rewrote the Declaration of Independence until every word was just right.

The Declaration of Independence said, "All men are created equal." Being born into a wealthy or powerful family did not give someone the right to rule others. Every person was born with the right to life, liberty, and the pursuit of happiness. Nobody could take these basic human rights away. In fact, government had a duty to protect these rights.

The Declaration also said that the people could choose new leaders if their own government did not serve them. The king of Britain had not protected the rights of the colonists, so the colonists had the right to start a new government.

After several days of discussion, members of the Congress approved Jefferson's draft of the Declaration. The Declaration of Independence was adopted by the Congress on July 4, 1776. It sent a strong message to Britain. America had the right to be free.

Jefferson left the Congress in autumn 1776. Back home, he served in the Virginia legislature. He also spent time at his beloved Monticello with his growing family. His daughter Martha had been born in 1772. Sadly, the next daughter, Jane, died before age two. His only son lived less than a month. Mary was born in 1778.

JEFFERSON AND SLAVERY

The Continental Congress did make some changes to Jefferson's Declaration. They took out a section he wrote against slavery. Jefferson himself owned slaves. They worked on the family plantation. But he believed that slavery was wrong and should be outlawed.

Jefferson had hoped to spend more time at Monticello. But in 1779, he was called to serve in a new role. The people of Virginia had elected him as their governor. One of his jobs was to protect Virginians from British attacks during the Revolutionary War. This was not always possible. Once, British troops almost captured him at Monticello, but he escaped.

Thomas Jefferson's wife, Martha, died a few months after her sixth child was born.

During these difficult years, the Jeffersons had a fourth daughter, Lucy. She died months later. Then Jefferson's wife, his pretty and sweet-tempered Martha, died in September 1782. She died after giving birth to a baby girl. The baby, also named Lucy, survived.

Jefferson was sick with grief over the loss of his wife. His oldest child, Martha, tried to comfort him during those dark days. All Jefferson wanted to do was lock himself in his room at Monticello and never leave. But he couldn't hide forever.

The colonies needed him. The Colonial army was struggling to win the war that would earn their freedom. They had won some important battles. And France had joined them, sending money and troops. For the first time, victory seemed near.

Dear Daughters,

Today I saw some of the most extraordinary

Bright red fruit that can be turned into the

Gia... ...lloons filled with a gas called heliu...

I ... ...ed into some of the most amaz...

4 GOVERNMENT BY THE PEOPLE

The American Revolution finally
ended in 1783. A new nation, the
United States, was born. Jefferson had
many hopes and dreams for his country. He
especially hoped it would be a true
democracy with government by the people.

Busy as ever, Jefferson divided his time between Congress and Monticello. At Monticello, he urged his daughters to spend their time wisely. A daily schedule he wrote for Martha listed music lessons, dancing, drawing, letter writing, French lessons, and reading. When he was away from home, he wrote many letters to his children. In one letter, he asked Martha to keep his letters and read them again. He believed this would help them to stay close.

Jefferson's daughter Martha could not always keep up with all the letters her father sent her. Sometimes Jefferson scolded her for not writing back.

The family was separated again when Jefferson was asked to become an ambassador to Europe. In the spring of 1784, he sailed to France with Martha. His other two daughters, Mary and young Lucy, stayed in America.

As an ambassador, Jefferson represented the government of the United States. He made agreements called treaties between the United States and other countries. He discussed how they would trade goods with each other. He gained the respect of the French, as well as people in Italy, Germany, and Belgium.

American artist John Trumbull came to Paris to paint this portrait of Thomas Jefferson at the age of forty-four.

PANCAKES AND TOMATOES

Jefferson experienced many new things in Europe. In Paris, he was thrilled to see men soar hundreds of feet in the sky in a gas-filled balloon. In Italy, he discovered a new favorite food—macaroni. He may have been the first American to taste a tomato. He also discovered the wonders of pancakes and of ice cream.

Jefferson also found time to visit Europe's museums and theaters and to attend concerts. He especially loved all the bookstores. By then, he owned thousands of books, and he bought hundreds more in Europe.

As much as Jefferson enjoyed life in Europe, he missed his family. In the fall, Jefferson's two-year-old daughter, Lucy, died from illness. Again, he grieved the loss of a loved one. He asked nine-year-old Mary to join him and Martha in Paris.

President Washington and four of his advisers. FROM LEFT TO RIGHT: George Washington, Henry Knox, Alexander Hamilton, Thomas Jefferson, and Edmund Randolph.

In 1789, Jefferson left France. When he returned home, he learned that there was another important job waiting for him. President George Washington wanted him to become the nation's first secretary of state.

As secretary of state, Jefferson built relationships between the United States and other countries. He also helped President Washington make decisions about the government.

Jefferson respected President Washington. Still, he was growing unhappy with the government. America had come a long way since the rule of the British king. People had more rights than ever. But Jefferson believed they should have even more. He thought a small group of landowners and other wealthy people held too much power. These people did not trust regular Americans to make important decisions. They wanted to choose the nation's leaders themselves. Jefferson argued that this was not a true democracy, with government for all the people.

Thomas Jefferson did not get along with Alexander Hamilton (right). The two men had very different ideas about how to run the government.

People who agreed with Jefferson formed a new political party called the Democratic Republicans. Jefferson became the leader of this party. He also decided to quit his job as secretary of state. He was ready to go home.

In January 1794, Jefferson returned to Monticello. As always, he got up early and was busy all day. He told friends that he rose with the sun.

Jefferson designed his bedroom to let in plenty of sunshine.

In his pockets, Jefferson carried all sorts of tools for writing and measuring things. He never knew when he might need them.

At age fifty, Jefferson still stood straight and slender. People commented on his sprightly step. Jefferson wore plain, comfortable clothes. In his pockets, he still carried a small notebook and pencil, as well as a compass, thermometer, and small set of scales for measuring things.

At Monticello, Jefferson worked to strengthen the Democratic Republican Party. He also spent many hours reading, writing, and adding features to his home.

The gardens and farmland that surrounded Monticello kept Jefferson and his slaves busy.

Outdoors, Jefferson worked hard to increase his crops. He needed to earn more money. His wife's father had left him large debts along with another plantation. Despite the problems, he loved being home. He once said that his farm, his family, his books, and his building projects, gave him more pleasure than any public office.

Jefferson thought he would remain at Monticello the rest of his life. But three years later, he agreed to serve his country once again. This time, he became vice president under President John Adams.

By the end of the 1700s, Jefferson had already given most of his life to his country. He did not like the arguments that were part of political life. But he felt strongly that the government should be for the people. He wanted to find a way to make sure his ideas were heard. He decided the best way would be to run for president of the United States.

5 THE PEOPLE'S FRIEND

Thomas Jefferson was elected president in 1800. On Inauguration Day, he wore a plain suit of clothing. And he did not ride in a fancy carriage as Washington and Adams had done.

President Jefferson said he wanted to make the nation more democratic. America belonged to the common people, not only the wealthy. From his first day in office, he hoped to set a new example.

As president, Jefferson helped the country grow. In 1803, he arranged for the United States to buy the land between the Mississippi River and the Rocky Mountains. The United States paid France fifteen million dollars for this Louisiana Territory. Because of the Louisiana Purchase, the nation doubled in size.

Thomas Jefferson as the third president of the United States

Lewis and Clark learned about the West by talking to the Native Americans who already lived there.

Jefferson also encouraged exploration of the land beyond the Mississippi. He wondered about the people, animals, and plants that lived there. He sent explorers Meriwether Lewis and William Clark on a voyage of discovery.

Around the time that Lewis and Clark set out on their adventure, Jefferson's daughter Mary died. The president said he felt as though he had lost half of everything he had. Now only Martha was left. At least Martha often joined him in Washington, D.C., with her husband. She kept her father company and served as his hostess when he had guests for dinner.

By the time his second term was over, Jefferson was ready to leave office. He could have tried to get elected again. But Jefferson thought eight years was long enough for one person to be president.

Jefferson returned to Monticello in March 1809. His home had grown to include thirty-five rooms and many new inventions. These inventions made life easier. Dumbwaiters, machines he first saw in France, carried wine up from the basement. Jefferson's closet had another machine to turn the racks of clothing. Skylights brought more light into the rooms.

Jefferson bought this machine to make copies of important papers. While he wrote with one pen, the other pen followed along on another sheet of paper.

Jefferson also devoted many hours to growing his garden. He once said, "No occupation is so delightful to me as the culture of the earth." His kitchen garden sat on the sunny southern slope of Monticello. There he grew about seventy kinds of vegetables and herbs. There were also fields of corn, wheat, tobacco, vegetables, and other crops. He sent parts of his favorite plants and trees to friends to grow in their gardens.

A GREEN THUMB

Jefferson liked to experiment in his garden and on his farm. Through the years, he tried new ways of farming and worked to improve the soil. One of his methods was to plant different crops in different years. He even invented a new kind of plow. He also planted seeds from many places, including the areas Lewis and Clark explored. The year he died, Jefferson was still trying out new kinds of plants.

ONIONS

TOMATO

MAGIC BEANS

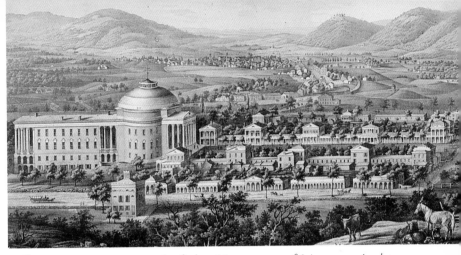

Jefferson was very proud of the University of Virginia. In his retirement, he designed its buildings, gardens, and classes.

Best of all, Jefferson watched his family grow. By then, he had at least twelve grandchildren and enjoyed playing with them. Sometimes they went horseback riding or planted flowers together. His granddaughter Ellen later said that Jefferson seemed to be able to read his grandchildren's hearts.

Even though he was retired, Jefferson continued to study, write, and serve his country. Members of the government and the public visited their beloved former president. And many people wrote to him. More than a thousand letters were sent to Jefferson, and he usually wrote back.

During his final years, Jefferson said he was pleased with his life. He said he had been blessed with good health and a loving family. He was thankful that he had been useful to his country and that people appreciated his work.

Thomas Jefferson died at age eighty-three on July 4, 1826. That very day marked the fifty-year anniversary of the Declaration of Independence.

Nearly two hundred years later, people are still awed by Jefferson's many talents. He was a farmer, lawyer, inventor, and scientist. He knew much about art, music, mathematics, archaeology, and architecture. Jefferson spoke several languages and studied Native American languages during his later years. He served the United States government in many ways. He will always be remembered as a brilliant thinker who fought for America's independence with his words.

TIMELINE

In the year . . .

1757 Tom's father, Peter Jefferson, died. **Age 14**

1760 he entered William and Mary College.

1762 he began to study law with George Wythe.

1768 he started building Monticello. **Age 25**

1769 he became a representative in the Virginia House of Burgesses.

1772 he married Martha Wayles Skelton on January 1.

1775 the Revolutionary War began on April 19. he attended the Second Continental Congress. **Age 32**

1776 he wrote the Declaration of Independence.

1779 he was elected governor of Virginia.

1782 his wife, Martha, died on September 6.

1784 he sailed to Europe. his daughter Lucy died. **Age 41**

1789 he left France for America.

1790 he became secretary of state under President George Washington.

1797 he became vice president under President John Adams. **Age 54**

1801 he became the third president of the United States.

1803 the Louisiana Territory was purchased. **Age 60**

1804 his daughter Mary died on April 17. Lewis and Clark began their expedition.

1809 he retired from public office.

1819 he founded the University of Virginia.

1826 he died on July 4. **Age 83**

SIGNERS OF THE DECLARATION

Fifty-six people signed the Declaration of Independence, and each signer had his own style. John Hancock took up a lot of room *(third column)*. The rebel Samuel Adams squeezed his name into a tiny space *(sixth column)*. What about Thomas Jefferson? Can you find his signature? Here's a clue: his name appears near the signature of his old law teacher, George Wythe.

FURTHER READING

NONFICTION

January, Brendan. *The Revolutionary War.* Danbury, CT: Children's Press, 2000. A photo-illustrated overview of the American Revolution.

Moore, Kay. *If You Lived at the Time of the American Revolution.* New York: Scholastic, 1998. Answers questions about what life was like, especially for children, during the Revolutionary War.

Quiri, Patricia Ryon. *The Declaration of Independence.* Danbury, CT: Children's Press, 1999. A photo-illustrated history of the Declaration of Independence.

Young, Robert. *A Personal Tour of Monticello.* Minneapolis: Lerner Publications Company, 1999. A photo-illustrated, firsthand account of Jefferson's beloved home.

FICTION

Fleming, Candace. *Big Cheese for the White House: The True Tale of A Tremendous Cheddar.* New York: DK Publishing, 1999. The story of a 1,235-pound cheese from Cheshire, Massachusetts, that was given to President Jefferson as a New Year's Day gift.

Fleming, Candace. *The Hatmaker's Sign: A Story by Benjamin Franklin.* New York: Orchard Books, 1998. While members of the Continental Congress tear apart Thomas Jefferson's draft of the Declaration of Independence, Benjamin Franklin tells his friend a tall tale to cheer him up.

WEBSITES

The Declaration of Independence
<www.nara.gov/exhall/charters/declaration/declaration.html> This website contains the exact wording of this document and the list of people who signed it.

The Official Monticello Web Site
<www.monticello.org> A chance to visit Jefferson's home online and learn more about America's third president.

Thomas Jefferson
<www.whitehouse.gov/history/presidents/tj3.html> Information about Thomas Jefferson on the White House's official website.

SELECT BIBLIOGRAPHY

Bear, James A. *Jefferson at Monticello*. Charlottesville, VA: University Press of Virginia, 1967.

Bober, Natalie S. *Thomas Jefferson: Man on a Mountain*. New York: Atheneum, 1988.

Kaminski, John P., ed. *Citizen Jefferson: The Wit and Wisdom of an American Sage*. Madison, WI: Madison House, 1994.

Larson, Martin A. *Jefferson, Magnificent Populist*. Washington, D.C.: Robert D. Luce, 1981.

Randall, Willard Sterne. *Thomas Jefferson: A Life*. New York: Henry Holt, 1993.

INDEX

Acknowledgments

For photographs and artwork: © Bettmann/Corbis, p. 4; © Monticello/Thomas Jefferson Foundation, Inc., pp. 7, 24, 33, 34, 39; © North Wind Picture Archives, pp. 8, 13, 17, 45; © Library of Congress, pp. 9, 11, 22, 30; © Independent Picture Service, p. 10 © Massachusetts Historical Society, p. 15; © Collection of the Maryland Historical Society, Baltimore, p. 18; © Manuscripts Print Collection, Special Collections Department, University of Virginia Library, pp. 21; © Diplomatic Reception Rooms, United States Department of State, p. 27; © White House Historical Association, p. 28; © Independence National Historical Park, p. 31; © Charlotsville Albemarle Convention and Visitors Bureau, p. 32; © Bowdoin College Museum of Art, Brunswick, Maine, Bequest of the Honorable James Bowdoin III, p. 37; © Hulton|Archive/Getty Images, p. 38; © Special Collections, University of Virginia Library, p. 41; © American Philosophical Society, p. 42. Front and back cover © Independence National Historical Park; front cover background © National Archives.

For quoted material: All quotations that appear in this book are the exact words of Thomas Jefferson, collected in *Citizen Jefferson: The Wit and Wisdom of an American Sage*. John P. Kaminiski, ed. Madison, WI: Madison House, 1994.